PEGASUS ENCYCLOPEDIA LIBRARY

World History
ANCIENT HISTORY

Edited by: Tapasi De, Pallabi B. Tomar
Managing editor: Tapasi De
Designed by: Vijesh Chahal, Anil Kumar and Rohit Kumar
Illustrated by: Suman S. Roy, Tanoy Choudhury
Colouring done by: Vinay Kumar, Sonu, Kiran Kumari & Pradeep Kumar

CONTENTS

The Ancient world 3

Mesopotamians and Sumerians 4

The Hittites and Assyrians 8

Land of River Nile – Egypt 10

Romans in Ancient Times 15

Beginning of Greek Civilisation 18

The Olmecs and the Chavins 22

The Ancient Arab World 25

Indus Valley Civilization 27

Ancient Africa 28

Test Your Memory 31

Index 32

The Ancient world

> It was in the ancient times that man learnt the use of stone tools, fire and then the art of farming. With the passage of time, civilizations came into being.

The Neolithic period or the New Stone Age was a period marked by a transition from hunting and gathering culture to settled farming. This transition allowed people to create permanent towns and villages and it paved the way to a more complex society and culture.

As the people no longer had to go in search of food, they could spend more time in other activities. They began experimenting with crafts like pottery and weaving. In addition to growing crops, these early humans also started domesticating animals to work for them and to serve as sources of food.

The beginning of permanent settlements brought about some other major changes as well. The concept of property (private or personal) and land ownership came into being. The concept of money began to emerge and some societies unfortunately started keeping slaves too.

The practice of religion and politics also became more complex. The Neolithic people also began to trade with each other and developed complex uses for animal products like wool and milk. The events of the Neolithic period prepared the ancient humans for the future ages when metals began to be used.

Mesopotamians and Sumerians

One of the earliest civilizations that ever existed in the ancient world was the Mesopotamian civilization which flourished between the river Euphrates and Tigris. Mesopotamia meant in Greek 'the land between the two rivers'. This portion of the land is now modern Iraq.

Mesopotamia consisted of largely independent city-states with their own typical religions, languages, kings and administrations. These city-states were always on the look-out for an opportunity for independence.

Ziggurat

A ziggurat is a temple tower of ancient Mesopotamian valley which was in the form of a terraced pyramid of successively receding storeys. Ziggurats were a form of temple common to the Sumerians, Babylonians and Assyrians of ancient Mesopotamia. The ziggurats were not places for public worship or ceremonies. They were believed to be dwelling places of the gods.

The earliest examples of the ziggurat date from the end of the third millennium BCE and the latest date from the 6th century BCE.

Built in receding tiers upon a rectangular, oval or square platform, the ziggurat was a pyramidal structure. Sun-baked

Mesopotamians and Sumerians

bricks made up the central part of the ziggurat. The facings were often glazed in different colours and may have had astrological significance. The number of tiers ranged from two to seven. Some notable examples of this structure include the Great Ziggurat of Ur and Khorsabad in Mesopotamia.

The Sumerians

It so happened that a group of early settlers wandered into this land between the two rivers, Euphrates and Tigris. The new settlers quickly took over as they were real pioneers. They built permanent homes of sun-dried bricks made of mud and straw and started a new life in the southern region of ancient Mesopotamia. These highly advanced people who began to develop a civilization on the land between two rivers are known as the Sumerians.

The Sumerian civilization probably began around 5000 BCE. In the beginning, they were an agricultural community. They grew crops and stored food for times of need.

Sumerian inventions

The ancient Sumerians were the inventors of many useful articles. Some of them were the wheel, the sailboat, the first written language, frying pans, razors, cosmetic sets, shepherd's pipes, harps, kilns to cook bricks and pottery, bronze hand tools like hammers and axes, the plow and the plow-seeder.

> There were four main classes of people in ancient Sumer— the priests, the upper class, the lower class, and the slaves.

Ziggurat

Gilgamesh

The ancient Sumerians were great story-tellers. Thousands of years ago, they created the story of Gilgamesh. Gilgamesh is said to be one of the oldest recorded stories in the world. It's about an ancient King of Uruk Gilgamesh.

According to the story, Gilgamesh was the first superhero! He was partly god and partly human. He had many special powers too.

Beginning of monarchy

The world's first system of monarchy was also invented by the Sumerians. The early Sumerian states needed a new form of government to govern larger areas and diverse people of their land. The states of Sumer were ruled by a priest-king whose duties included leading the military, trade, judging disputes and taking part in vital religious ceremonies. Under the priest-king were several priests who surveyed land, assigned fields and distributed the harvest. The monarch was considered to be divine and were expected to be worshipped.

Cities

The ancient Sumerians built many cities along the Tigris and the Euphrates Rivers. Archaeologists believe that their largest city, the city of Ur, had a population of around 24,000 residents.

Cuneiform

Developing a system of writing is perhaps the most significant among all the Sumerian inventions. It helped the Sumerians to communicate, contribute to literature and also assisted in keeping records. Cuneiform was the first form of writing developed by the Sumerians around 3200 BC. Clay tablets were used as paper. The Sumerians scrawled their picture words using reeds on wet clay which would then dry into stone-hard tablets. These clay tablets were then baked for preservation. Early Sumerian writing was pictographic writing.

Astronomy

Another very remarkable Sumerian invention comprises of the invention of the calendar. Based on the cycle of the moon, the Sumerians invented the calendar which was divided into twelve months. Since a year consisting of twelve lunar months was shorter than a solar year, the Sumerians also added a 'leap year' every three years to catch up with the sun.

Mesopotamians and Sumerians

Sumerian religion

The Sumerians believed that the world was created out of an ancient sea from where the universe, gods and the people were created. They believed that the universe was ruled by these gods, who were anthropomorphic (they had human features and personalities). Each Sumerian city-state had its own patron deity to whom the citizens paid homage. Temples known as ziggurats were often erected in the cities to honour and house each city's god. The city of Ur, for example, constructed a ziggurat for Nanna, the God of the Moon.

The most important gods of the Sumerians were Enki (God of Water), Ki (God of Earth), Enlil (God of Air), and An (God of Heaven). These main gods were believed to have created the rules of Sumerian society which all people were expected to follow. Sumerians also believed that the reason for their existence was to delight the gods. Rituals and animal sacrifices were considered necessary in order to satisfy these deities.

Art and Craft

The Sumerians were wonderful craftsmen. They made jewellery of precious gold and lapis, fancy chairs and unglazed vases that kept water cool. They created colourful mosaics in intricate and beautiful patterns using little pieces of painted clay. Archaeologists have found remains of their mosaics, helmets, harps, jewellery, pottery and decorated tablets. They made beautiful pottery from wet soil. It has been found that the Sumerians used many musical instruments including the harp, reed pipes, drums and the lyre.

The Sumerians learned to build levees across the Euphrates and Tigris which helped them to store water.

The Hittites and Assyrians

Hittities

The Hittites ruled a great empire that stretched from Mesopotamia to Syria and Palestine. The origin of the Hittites is shrouded in mystery. The Hittites are perhaps one of the most significant people in Mesopotamian history. As their primary activity was trading with all the civilizations of the Mediterranean, the Hittites spread the Mesopotamian thought, law, political structure, economic structure and ideas around the Mediterranean, from Egypt to Greece.

Law: The Hittites greatly modified the system of law they inherited from the Old Babylonians. These laws were far more merciful than the laws of the Old Babylonians. Under the Hittites, only a small handful of crimes got capital punishments.

Religion: The Hittites worshipped many of the gods of the Sumerians and the Old Babylonians. Whenever they conquered some people, they adopted the gods of those people into their religious system.

The Assyrians

For hundreds of years the Assyrians occupied a territory that was bordered by extremely powerful civilizations. As a result, the Assyrians were frequently attacked by their neighbours. The constant threat of attack led the Assyrians to develop the most powerful army in the region. Once the army was made, the Assyrians began attacking and conquering the people who once threatened them. As they did so, they earned a reputation of extreme cruelty to those whom they conquered. By 650 B.C. the Assyrians had conquered a vast empire, stretching between the Persian Gulf, the Red Sea, the Mediterranean Sea, the Black Sea and the Caspian Sea.

Mathematics and science: It is a striking fact that Assyrian culture had a dramatic growth in science and mathematics. Among the great mathematical inventions of the Assyrians was the division of the circle into 360 degrees. They were among the first to invent longitude and latitude required in geographical navigation. They also developed a highly advanced medical science which greatly influenced the medical science of Greece also.

Trade and Commerce: In the Assyrian cities, long docks were built along the sides of the rivers so that ships could easily unload the goods they had to trade with. Ships brought food, drinks, clothes, jewellery, wine and other goods.

The Assyrians, who lived in northern Mesopotamia were famous traders. They did not use boats to move their goods.

The Hittites and Assyrians

They travelled on land. The ancient Mesopotamians did not have a lot of natural resources. They counted on trade to obtain the goods they needed.

Art and craft: The Assyrians were not that interested in art for the sake of beauty. They used art to display huge scenes of their military achievements and the daily life of the military people when they were not at war. There are also murals of the royal people and their activities. We know a great deal about the Assyrians because of the pictures of their daily life they carved and painted.

Astonishing fact

The last Assyrian king had started a project. He began collecting a library of clay tablets of all the literature of Sumer, Babylon and Assyria. No one knows how many tablets he actually collected, but when this library was discovered in modern times, over 30,000 tablets still remained in the great library at Nineveh, his capital city!

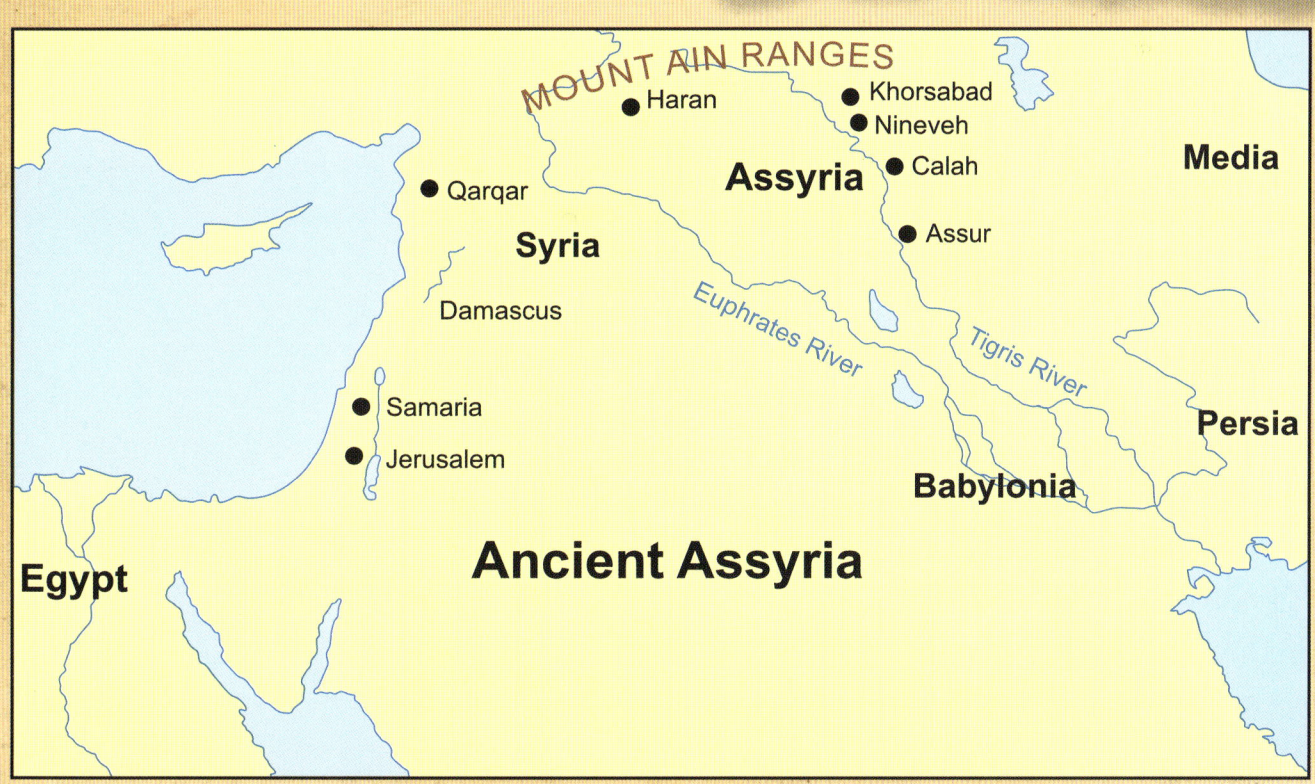

Land of River Nile – Egypt

River Nile

Sphinx

The ancient Egyptians believed that Egypt was divided into two types of land—the 'black land' and the 'red land'.

The 'black land' was the fertile land on the banks of the Nile.

The 'red land' was believed to be a barren desert that protected Egypt from both the sides. These deserts separated ancient Egypt from neighbouring countries and invasions.

Egyptian life

River Nile formed the life-blood of Egypt. Daily life in ancient Egypt revolved around the Nile and its fertile banks. The yearly flooding of the Nile enriched the soil and brought good harvests to the land.

The people of ancient Egypt built homes made of mud bricks. They grew some of their own food and traded for the goods

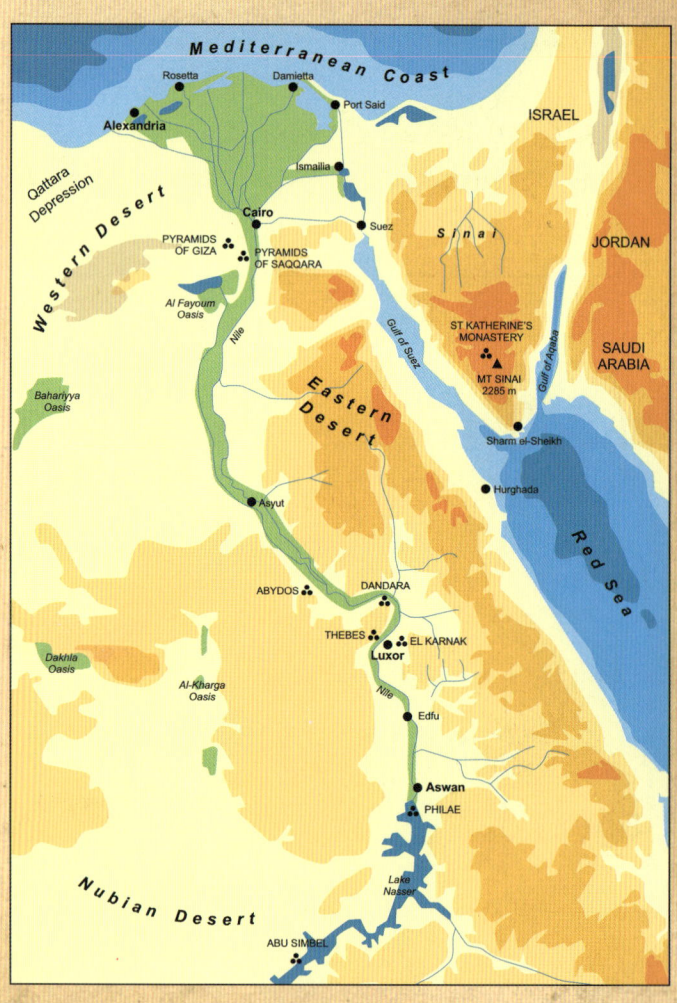

Land of River Nile – Egypt

they could not produce. Most ancient Egyptians worked as farmers, craftsmen and scribes. A small group of people were nobles. Together, these different groups of people made up the population of ancient Egypt.

Astonishing fact

Both Egyptian men and women wore make up. Eye paint was commonly applied— green (made from copper) was used by females and black (made from lead) was used by males. In ancient Egyptian culture, it was believed that eye paint protected the eyes from harmful sun's rays.

Religion

The ancient Egyptians believed in many different gods and goddesses. One of the most important Egyptian gods were Ra—the Sun God offered protection and some took care of the people after they died.

Mummification

The earliest ancient Egyptians buried their dead in small pits in the desert. The heat and dryness of the sand dehydrated the bodies quickly, creating lifelike, natural 'mummies'.

Ra

Later, the ancient Egyptians began burying their dead in coffins to protect them from animals in the desert. However, they realised that bodies placed in coffins decayed soon.

Over many centuries, the ancient Egyptians developed a method of preserving bodies so that they would remain lifelike. They embalmed the bodies and wrapping them in strips of linen. Today we call this process **mummification**.

ANCIENT HISTORY

Pharaohs

The most powerful person in ancient Egypt was the pharaoh. The pharaoh was the political and religious leader of the Egyptian people. He owned all of the land, made laws, collected taxes and defended Egypt against foreigners. He performed rituals and built temples to honour the gods.

There are about eighty pyramids known to have existed in ancient Egypt. The three largest and the best-preserved of these were built at Giza. The most well-known of these pyramids was built for the Pharaoh Khufu. It is known as the 'Great Pyramid'.

Temples

The ancient Egyptians believed that temples were the homes of the

Pyramids of Egypt

The ancient Egyptians built pyramids as tombs for the pharaohs and their queens. The pharaohs were buried in the pyramids.

Temple of Luxor, Egypt

Astonishing fact

A pharaoh never let his hair down in a court room. He always covered his hair with a crown or a headdress called a nemes.

Pyramids

Land of River Nile – Egypt

gods and goddesses. Every temple was dedicated to a god or goddess and he or she was worshipped there by the temple priests and the pharaoh.

The large temple buildings were made of stone and their walls were covered with scenes that were carved on the stone and brightly painted. These scenes showed the pharaoh fighting in battles and performing rituals.

Abu Simbel Temples

Abu Simbel temples are two massive rock temples in Nubia in southern Egypt on the western bank of Lake Nasser. The twin temples were originally carved out of the mountainside during the reign of Pharaoh Ramesse II in the 13th century BC, as a lasting monument to himself and his Queen Nefertari. Interestingly, the complex was relocated entirely in the 1960s on an artificial hill high above the Aswan High Dam reservoir.

Hieroglyphics

The ancient Egyptians invented written scripts that could be used to record all information.

The most famous of all ancient Egyptian scripts is hieroglyphics. Hieroglyphs were represented in the form of symbols and pictures. They were mainly written on papyrus paper or on Pyramids. Hieroglyphics meant 'Writing the Words of

Abu Simbel Temple

God'. Throughout three thousand years of ancient Egyptian civilisation, at least three other scripts were also used for different purposes.

Tutankhamun

The most well-known Egyptian Pharaoh is without doubt, Tutankhamun.

Tutankhamun was probably born at Akhetaten which was the capital city of Egypt. He was born in about the year 1346 BC. His father was the pharaoh Akehenhaten.

Tutankhamun became the Pharaoh of Egypt soon after his father died in 1337 BC, when he was only nine years old.

Soon after he became pharaoh, he married

Tutankhamun with his wife

> One of the reasons why the Egyptians were able to develop an advanced civilization was because they were surrounded by deserts. This kept invaders out of their land.

his teenage sister. By the age of 19 he was dead.

What caused Tutankhamun's death has been the subject of considerable debate. Major studies have been conducted in an effort to establish the cause of death.

Romans in ancient times

Ancient Rome was a civilization that grew out of a small agricultural community on the Italian Peninsula as early as the 10th century BC. Located along the Mediterranean Sea, it became one of the largest and the most powerful empires in the ancient world.

Legend of Romulus and Remus

Romans believe that Rome was formed by two young boys called Romulus and Remus. The story goes like this. Rhea was married to Mars, the Roman God of War. They had twin sons. Once, she came to know that the other gods were to harm her family. To protect the sons, she floated them in the river, hoping someone would find them.

These young boys were found by a she-wolf who fed them. Later, a shepherd and his wife adopted the boys.

As the twins grew older, they decided that they did not want to take care of sheep but they wanted to be kings! They decided to build a city on the shores of river Tiber. As they both wanted to be the king, they quarrelled. In a fit of rage, Romulus killed his brother and made himself the king.

Roman architecture

One of the things the Romans are most famous for is their architecture. The Romans brought a lot of new ideas to architecture, of which the three most important are the arch, the baked brick and the use of cement and concrete.

The Romans built temples and basilicas, amphitheaters for gladiatorial games, Colosseum, Pantheon and Parthenon are evidences of their grand style and artistic sense.

Astonishing fact

The first-ever shopping mall was built by the Emperor Trajan in Rome. It consisted of several levels and more than 150 outlets that sold everything ranging from food and spices to clothes.

ANCIENT HISTORY

Colosseum

The ancient Romans were great builders. They built things so that they would last for centuries to come. The Colosseum was designed to host huge events. It was built of concrete, faced with stone as were most amphitheaters. It was built in the early days of the Roman Empire around 70 CE. Anyone could attend the events in the Colosseum. Admission was free.

The Colosseum could seat 45,000 spectators! This is where the ancient Romans gathered to watch the combat between gladiators, and battles between men and wild animals. On certain occasions, the Colosseum would be flooded with water to hold naval battles.

Julius Caesar

Julius Caesar was a great general and an important leader in ancient Rome. During his lifetime, he had held many important titles in the Roman Republic including that of a consul.

The people trusted him completely and they wanted to see Julius in a more powerful position.

As Julius Caesar became more popular with the people, the leaders in the Senate began to worry. And one day he was brutally murdered by all his senators and by one of his most trusted senator—Brutus.

Romans in ancient times

Gladiators

Gladiators were male slaves who were fearsome warriors. They were all professional fighters. Sometimes they were condemned criminals and prisoners of war. The successful gladiators received great acclaim. They were all forced to become swordsman. They would fight each other in amphitheatres. Sometimes the gladiators even fought with wild animals like lions, tigers, bears and bulls.

Roman Gods and Goddesses

The Romans believed in many different gods, goddesses and demigods (half-humans and half god) and spirits. They believed that each god had specific powers and controlled parts of the world. The main god was Jupiter. For each of the gods and goddesses, the Romans built temples. Priests looked after the temples and took part in the religious ceremonies. When people wanted to thank a god or a goddess they brought gifts of animals for sacrifice to the temple. Some of the important god and goddesses were Apollo (God of Music), Mars (God of War), Minerva (Goddess of Intelligence) and Venus (God of Love).

Christianity and Rome

During the first century CE, a new religion began in Rome. It was called Christianity. The followers of Christianity were called Christians. Christians believed in one god. They refused to worship the Roman gods. In ancient Rome, that was against the law. Christians were looked upon as criminals.

In spite of persecution, Christians grew in numbers rapidly. They told others about the benefits of being a Christian. They actively converted people into Christianity.

Rome's first university, La Sapienza is the largest in Europe and the second largest in the world.

Beginning of Greek Civilisation

Ancient Greece is called 'the birthplace of Western Civilisation'. About 2500 years ago, the Greeks created a way of life that other people admired and tried to emulate. The Ancient Greeks tried to enforce democracy, started the Olympic Games and left new ideas in science, art and philosophy.

Minoans and the Mycenaeans

About 3000 BC, there lived on the island of Crete a group of people now called Minoans. The name comes from their King, Minos. Minos and other Minoan kings grew rich from trade and built fine palaces. The Minoan civilization ended about 1450 BC.

After the Minoans came the Mycenaeans. They were basically soldiers from the mainland of Greece. It was the Mycenaean people who fought in Troy in the 1200s BC. After the Mycenaean age ended about 1100 BC, Greece entered a 'Dark Age'. This lasted until the 800s BC when the Greeks set off by sea to explore and set up colonies. Around 480 BC the 'Golden Age' of Greece began. This is what the historians call the 'Classical' age of Greece.

We get most of the information about Greece from three major ancient historians—Herodotus, known as the 'Father of History', Thucydides and Xenophon. Other sources include temples, sculpture, pottery, artifacts and other archaeological findings.

The Trojan War

The Trojans lived in the city of Troy, what is now modern Turkey. The Trojan War

In the valley of Olympia, the very first recorded Ancient Olympic contests were held in 776 B.C. Olympia lay within the city-state of Elis in a region of Ancient Greece known as Peloponnesus. Although, the actual beginning of the Olympic Games is not precisely known, but it was certainly connected with contests between gods and heroes.

Beginning of Greek Civilisation

began when Paris, the Prince of Troy, ran away with Helen, wife of King Menelaus of Sparta. The Greeks sent a fleet of ships with a huge army to get her back. The war lasted for 10 years. The Trojan War ended with the victory of the Greeks though by a clever trick— by using a wooden horse.

The Wooden Horse

The Greeks pretended to sail away one day, leaving behind a giant wooden horse. Inside the horse, Greek soldiers hid. Seeing that the Greeks had retreated, the Trojans rejoiced. They dragged the wooden horse into their city thinking it to be a gift.

That night the Greek ships returned. While the Trojans were asleep, the hidden Greeks climbed out of the wooden horse. They opened the city gates, and let in the Greek army. Troy was destroyed. The Trojan War was over.

ANCIENT HISTORY

Greek Gods and Goddesses

The Greeks were polytheistic in their religious beliefs. Their religion had no formal structure though they had festivals to honour the gods. There was no sacred book or code of conduct to live by.

The most powerful Greek Gods were known as the Olympians. The Greeks believed that the Olympians lived on the highest mountain in Greece, Mount Olympus. The Olympian gods included Zeus, Hera, Apollo, Aphrodite, Ares, Artemis, Athena, Demeter, Hades, Hermes, Hephaestus, Poseidon and Hestia.

Alexander the Great

Alexander the Great was the son of King Philip II of Macedonia. Alexander, at the age of twenty took over where Philip had left off and continued to expand their empire.

From the age of 13, Alexander was tutored by the famous Greek philosopher Aristotle. Alexander proved to be an incredible military commander. After years of warfare he had conquered a huge portion of the land. Everywhere he conquered, he spread the Greek language and culture.

In June 10 or 11, 323 B.C Alexander died of fever in Babylon at the age of 32. After his death, his kingdom was divided into three separate kingdoms ruled by the descendents of his generals.

Socrates

Socrates was one of the most famous philosophers of ancient Greece. He believed the quest for knowledge was more important than money. He never wrote down any of his teachings. Information about his life and teaching came from other philosophers and his students such as Plato.

Plato

Plato was a pupil of Socrates, the famous Greek scholar and teacher. Plato believed that a person should try to reach the 'ideal human state' through philosophy.

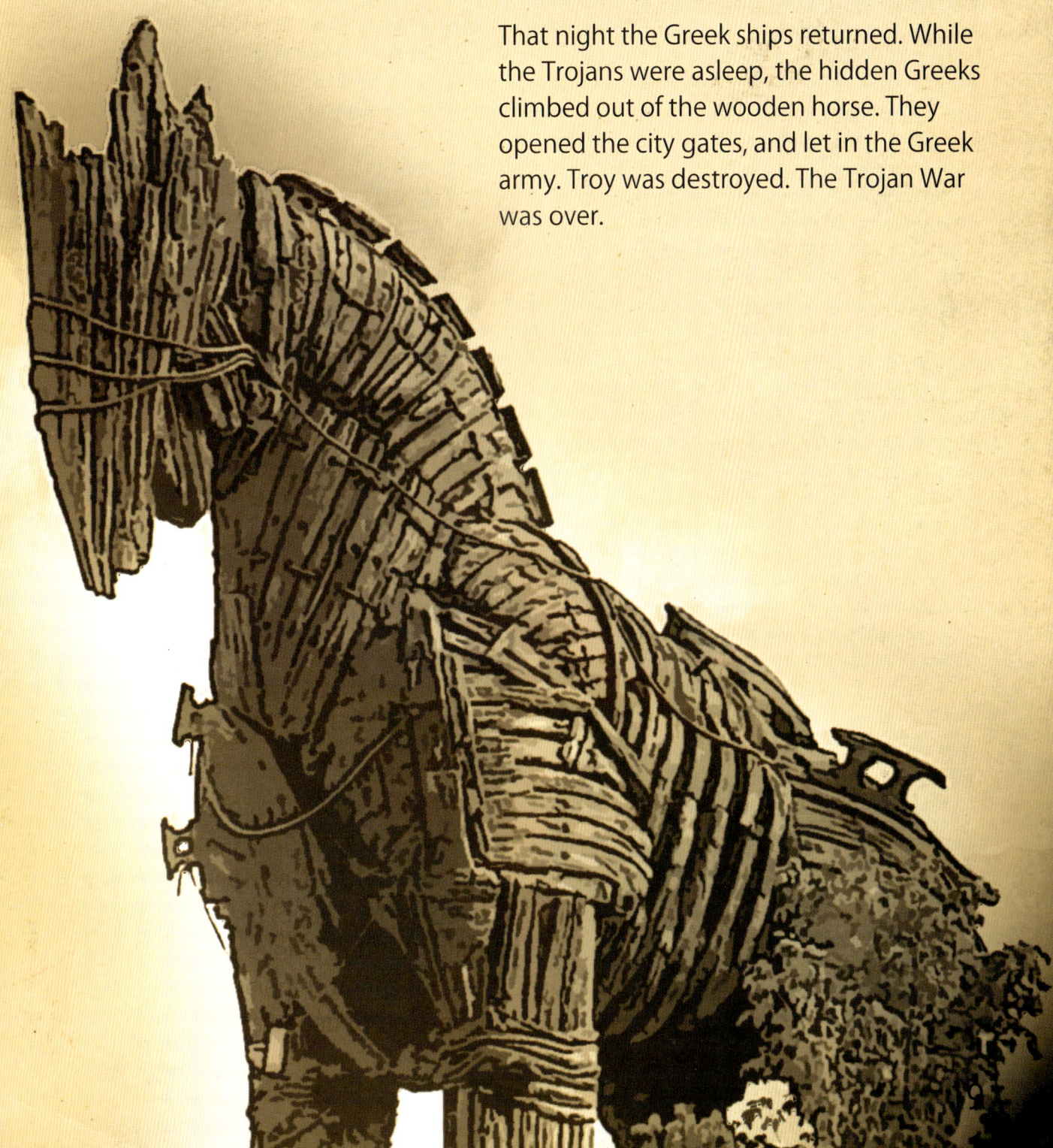

He believed that philosopher kings should rule city-states. His focus was to produce good men which would inevitably lead to a good state.

Aristotle

Aristotle was born in 384 B.C. He was a philosopher, politician, botanist and zoologist. He was a student of Plato. After studying under Plato for sometime, he tutored Alexander the Great. After tutoring Alexander for three years, Aristotle returned to Athens.

In Athens, he developed his own school, called the Lyceum. Aristotle was known to have written over five hundred books, of which only thirty have survived.

Athens

Athens was the largest and most powerful Greek state. It was a city full of splendid public buildings, shops and public baths. The people of Athens lived at the foothill of Acropolis, a rocky hill. The marble Parthenon, a temple, was built on the highest part of the Acropolis.

Athens did not have a king. It was ruled by the people as a democracy. The people of Athens chose their ruler. They held large meetings which was called the Assembly.

Sparta

The ancient Greek city of Sparta was well-known for having brave and fierce fighters.

Most Spartans were either Perioeci (citizens who paid taxes, served in the army and were protected by Spartan laws) or Helots (people from lands conquered and ruled by Sparta). The Helots were treated as serfs (slaves) and had to give half their crops to their Spartan master.

Parthenon

Parthenon was dedicated to the Greek Goddess Athena— the Goddess of Wisdom and War. Inside the Parthenon, stood a large statue of Athena made of gold and ivory. Athena was the patron of the city of Athens.

Panthenon

The Olmecs and the Chavins

The first inhabitants of the American continents were nomadic hunters and gatherers. These nomads probably arrived in North America around 40,000 years ago. As these various groups travelled into the new world, they spread out across the land, forming new cultures and sometimes complex civilizations. For four thousand years, these early inhabitants of the Americas made a life by hunting and gathering food.

Then around 5000 B.C. an agricultural revolution took place near the present day Mexico. They realized that they could plant crops such as corn, pumpkins, potatoes and squash. New religions and governments began to form.

Cultural differentiation

The various peoples living in North America gradually developed many different and unique cultures. Each culture was influenced by the land and natural resources around the people. These cultures included their traditions, religious practices and their everyday lives and customs.

Mesoamerican Cultures

The people who inhabited Central America formed a number of advanced civilizations between 1500 B.C. and A.D. 1200. As one civilization faded in this region, another developed.

Historians call these civilizations the Mesoamerican cultures. The word 'meso' means 'middle'.

The Olmecs

The first civilization to evolve in Mesoamerica was that of the Olmecs. Around 1500 B.C. villages in Mesoamerica became more complex and specialized. These people formed a nation which they called Olmec.

Mesoamerican highlands

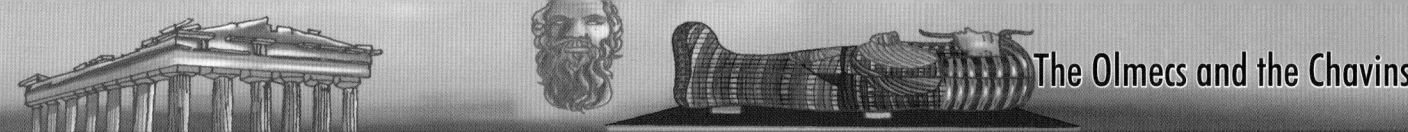

The Olmecs and the Chavins

The Olmecs built huge religious stone emblems of their gods and rulers. Some of these emblems were more than 9 ft tall, and weighed more than 40 tons!

The Olmec villages had a market square in the centre where trade took place. They worshiped many gods and deities. Their chief god was believed to be a god with a human body and a jaguar face.

The Olmecs were expert farmers, and practiced a type of farming known as 'slash-and-burn' farming. They would cut down the trees of a forest and wait for a period of several months for the trees to dry out. They would then set the trees on fire burning them all into ashes. These ashes acted as a fertilizer making the soil more fertile. These farmers then farmed the land for a few years until it was no longer fertile. Then they moved on to the next forest.

Chavin

Among all the civilization in the Peruvian prehistory, the best known is Chavin. The Chavin culture existed in the area what is now the modern state of Peru. Chavin is one of Peru's oldest civilizations and laid the cultural foundations of all later Peruvian civilizations. The Chavin culture flourished from 900 BCE to 200 BCE.

Olmec stone head

Chavin pottery

ANCIENT HISTORY

The Chavin culture is known for its beautiful arts and designs. Chavin designs can be appreciated only as abstract patterns, and there is almost always a hidden significance behind them. They were also innovative with metallurgy and textile production. Chavin art bears some quite some resemblance to Olmec art suggesting that there may have been some influence between the two cultures.

Spiritual meeting place of the Chavins

Chavin art

The Ancient Arab World

Arabia is the name of the country which lies to the west and south of Mesopotamia, a vast arid desert and the birthplace of Islam. We don't know much about these people because not much archaeological activity has been done yet in the Arabian Peninsula (modern Saudi Arabia, Yemen, Qatar, Oman and the United Arab Emirates). But from what ever little information that we have now, it is clear that these people had a thriving civilization that was reasonably old.

The south-western part of the Arabian Peninsula gets more rain than the north or the east. So people began farming there more than in the other areas. In the north and the east of the Arabian Peninsula most people did not cultivate, because there wasn't enough rain. Instead, they became shepherds and herded sheep all around the peninsula.

The Nabataeans

The Nabataean were trading people of ancient Arabia. Their empire stretched from modern-day Yemen to Damascus and from western Iraq into the Sinai Desert according to some historians.

History tells us that the Nabataeans were nomads, dwelling in tents in the desert. Yet, within a few years they built spectacular and awe inspiring monuments. The magnificent city of Petra is such an example. This impressive city was hidden away in the cleft of a rock with an access through a narrow crack in a mountain. Thousands of monuments and tombs were erected in this hidden city. And then suddenly, one day the Nabataeans handed their empire over to the Romans soldiers and disappeared from the scene!

Who were these Nabataeans who suddenly appeared in history? Why did they build such extraordinary monuments and then disappear? These are only some of the questions that archeologists have been asking as they have dug through the sands of time.

ANCIENT HISTORY

Petra—the lost city

Petra is a unique 2000 year old rock-cut city in Jordan. It was established sometime around the 6th century BC as the capital city of the Nabataeans. The remains of the once lost Nabataean city of Petra includes temples, Roman theaters, monasteries, houses and roads. This ancient intriguing city flourished for over 400 years around the time of Rome and Christ, until it was occupied by the Roman Emperor Trajan in 106 A.D.

Carved on rock and protected by rocky mountains on all sides, Petra is Jordan's most famous tourist attraction. Lost to outsiders for hundreds of years, Petra has been a symbol of the hidden treasures of the Near East since its rediscovery in 1812 by the Swiss explorer John Ludwig Burckhardt.

The Holy City of Mecca

Mecca (Makkah in Arabic) is the centre of the Islamic world and the birthplace of both the Prophet Muhammad and the religion he founded. Located in the Sirat Mountains of central Saudi Arabia and 45miles inland from the Red Sea port of Jidda (Jeddah), ancient Mecca was an oasis on the old caravan trade route that linked the Mediterranean world with South Arabia, East Africa and South Asia.

Mecca

Indus Valley Civilization

The Indus Valley civilization was also known as the Harappan Civilization after the village named Harappa, which is now in Pakistan, where the civilization was first discovered. It is also known as the Indus Valley Civilization because two of its best-known cities, Harappa and Mohenjo-Daro, are situated along the banks of the Indus River.

This Indus Valley Civilization existed from about 3000-2,500 BCE to about 1500 BCE, which means it existed at about the same time as the Egyptian and Sumerian civilizations.

Houses

Houses in the Indus Valley were one or two storeys high, made of baked bricks with flat roofs. Each house was built around a courtyard. Each home had its own private drinking well and its own private bathroom! Clay pipes led from the bathrooms to sewers located under the streets.

Art

The Indus Valley Civilization must have had marvellous craftsmen, skilled in pottery, weaving and metal working. The pottery that has been found is of very high quality. Several small figures of animals, such as monkeys have been found along with small female statues. They have found bowls made of bronze and silver, and many beads and ornaments.

Great bath

In the ancient city of Mohenjo-Daro, scientists have found the remains of a large central pool, with steps leading down at both ends. Around this large central pool were smaller rooms that might have been dressing rooms.

Ancient Africa

The continent of Africa provides a varied landscape of forests, river valleys, deserts and grasslands. It is the place where people first originated. At first, about two million years ago, there may have been only about 2000 people in the whole of Africa, and they must have lived by gathering wild plants and by scavenging meat that other stronger animals killed. About 1.9 million years ago, they began using stone tools, and about 800,000 years ago they began to use fire. Cooking their food on the fire to make it easier to digest maybe what gave early people the extra energy to grow bigger brains and become modern people. These first modern people probably evolved in south-east Africa.

Nubia (Land of Gold)

The Kingdom of Kush or Nubia was located on the Nile River, to the south of ancient Egypt. Nubia was also known as the 'Land of the Bow' because their archers were expert and fierce. The army of archers kept the Nubian people safe. Many kingdoms wanted to control Nubia. It was a land of natural wealth. They had gold mines, ivory, incense and iron ore. Unlike Egypt, they were not dependent upon the flooding of the Nile for good soil. They enjoyed tropical rainfall all year long.

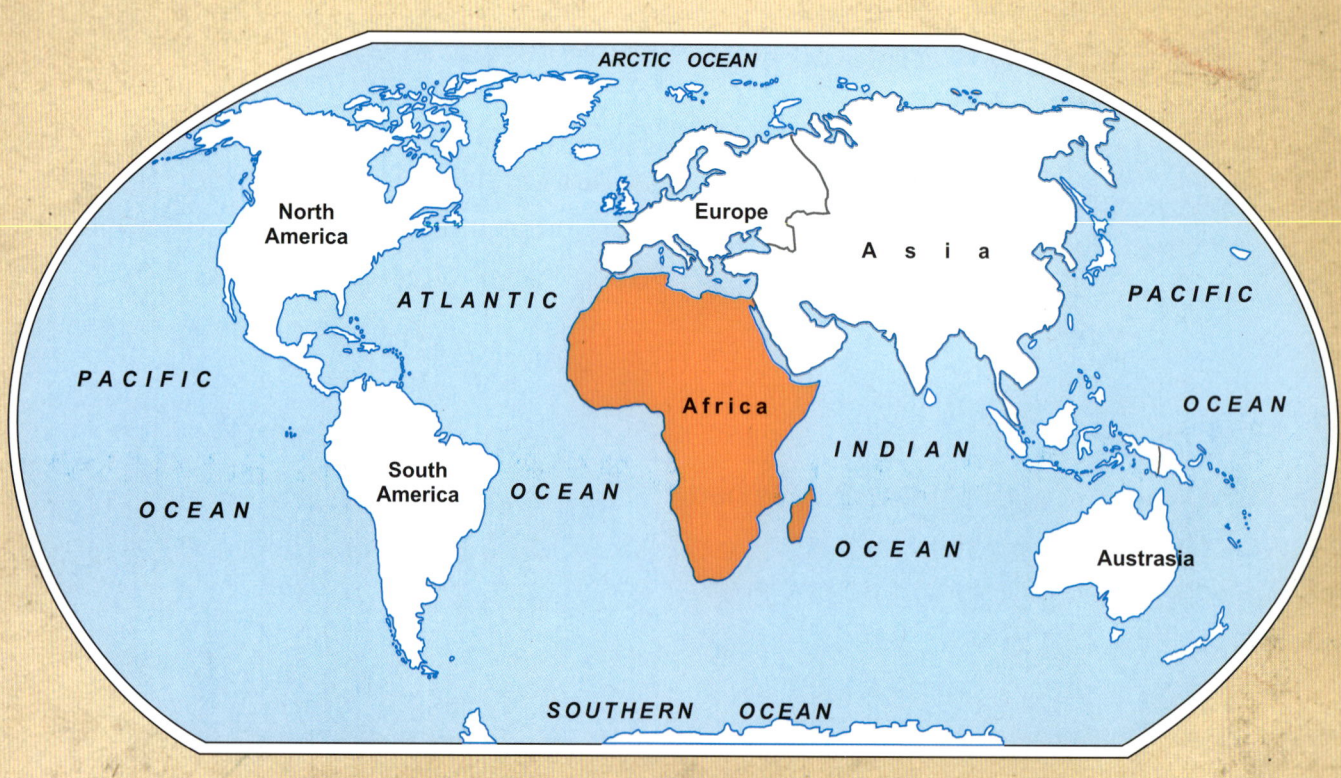

Ancient Africa

Inventions

African people made the earliest and the most important, scientific inventions. The earliest tools, the earliest use of fire and the earliest use of numbers are all from Africa. People in Africa began to make their own stone tools about 1.9 million years ago. Around 60,000 BC, African explorers left Africa and settled in India and Australia, and then West Asia, Europe, and China.

The Africans who stayed behind in Africa began to make fish-hooks, bows and arrows etc. By around 35,000 BC, African people were using tally sticks to keep track of numbers. Women were responsible for the early pottery industry, and also for iron smelting. Both women and men were involved in making African medicine.

Writing

Nobody really knows yet whether the Egyptians invented the art of writing for themselves, or whether they learned it from the Sumerians, who also began writing about the same time, about 3000 BC. The Egyptian form of writing, hieroglyphs, does not look the same or work the same as the Sumerian form of writing, cuneiform. So if they did get the idea from the Sumerians, the Egyptians certainly modified it a lot.

Astonishing fact

The ancient Africans believed in magic amulets. People would visit the village witchdoctor in hopes of finding help for their problems. The witchdoctor may have made them a magic amulet. It is not surprising that the people believed in magic as the amulets often worked!

Ancient African religion

The people in the ancient African villages believed that one god ruled the world, but many gods were in charge of daily life. They believed in two worlds – the world on Earth and the world of the gods. Their religion was designed to bring these two worlds together so that the elders, their religious leaders, could talk to the gods of daily life and receive advice. To encourage these gods to visit them, they danced, sang, rattled noisemakers, made masks and feasted.

Ancestor worship

The ancient Africans also asked their ancestors to talk to the gods on their behalf. They did many things to please their ancestors so that they would make a request on their behalf – things like storytelling and music and song and dance and feasting.

Ancient African Art

The earliest art we know about comes from South Africa, where there are carvings from about 80,000 BC. After that, however, there's a big gap. By about 27,000 BC, people in South Africa, may have been painting pictures of people and animals on rock walls.

African masks

African art

Astonishing fact

The term 'evil eye' is send to have originated in Africa. It is believed to bring harm to the sick and vulnerable.

Indus Valley Civilization

The Indus Valley civilization was also known as the Harappan Civilization after the village named Harappa, which is now in Pakistan, where the civilization was first discovered. It is also known as the Indus Valley Civilization because two of its best-known cities, Harappa and Mohenjo-Daro, are situated along the banks of the Indus River.

This Indus Valley Civilization existed from about 3000-2,500 BCE to about 1500 BCE, which means it existed at about the same time as the Egyptian and Sumerian civilizations.

Houses

Houses in the Indus Valley were one or two storeys high, made of baked bricks with flat roofs. Each house was built around a courtyard. Each home had its own private drinking well and its own private bathroom! Clay pipes led from the bathrooms to sewers located under the streets.

Art

The Indus Valley Civilization must have had marvellous craftsmen, skilled in pottery, weaving and metal working. The pottery that has been found is of very high quality. Several small figures of animals, such as monkeys have been found along with small female statues. They have found bowls made of bronze and silver, and many beads and ornaments.

Great bath

In the ancient city of Mohenjo-Daro, scientists have found the remains of a large central pool, with steps leading down at both ends. Around this large central pool were smaller rooms that might have been dressing rooms.

Ancient Africa

The continent of Africa provides a varied landscape of forests, river valleys, deserts and grasslands. It is the place where people first originated. At first, about two million years ago, there may have been only about 2000 people in the whole of Africa, and they must have lived by gathering wild plants and by scavenging meat that other stronger animals killed. About 1.9 million years ago, they began using stone tools, and about 800,000 years ago they began to use fire. Cooking their food on the fire to make it easier to digest maybe what gave early people the extra energy to grow bigger brains and become modern people. These first modern people probably evolved in south-east Africa.

Nubia (Land of Gold)

The Kingdom of Kush or Nubia was located on the Nile River, to the south of ancient Egypt. Nubia was also known as the 'Land of the Bow' because their archers were expert and fierce. The army of archers kept the Nubian people safe. Many kingdoms wanted to control Nubia. It was a land of natural wealth. They had gold mines, ivory, incense and iron ore. Unlike Egypt, they were not dependent upon the flooding of the Nile for good soil. They enjoyed tropical rainfall all year long.

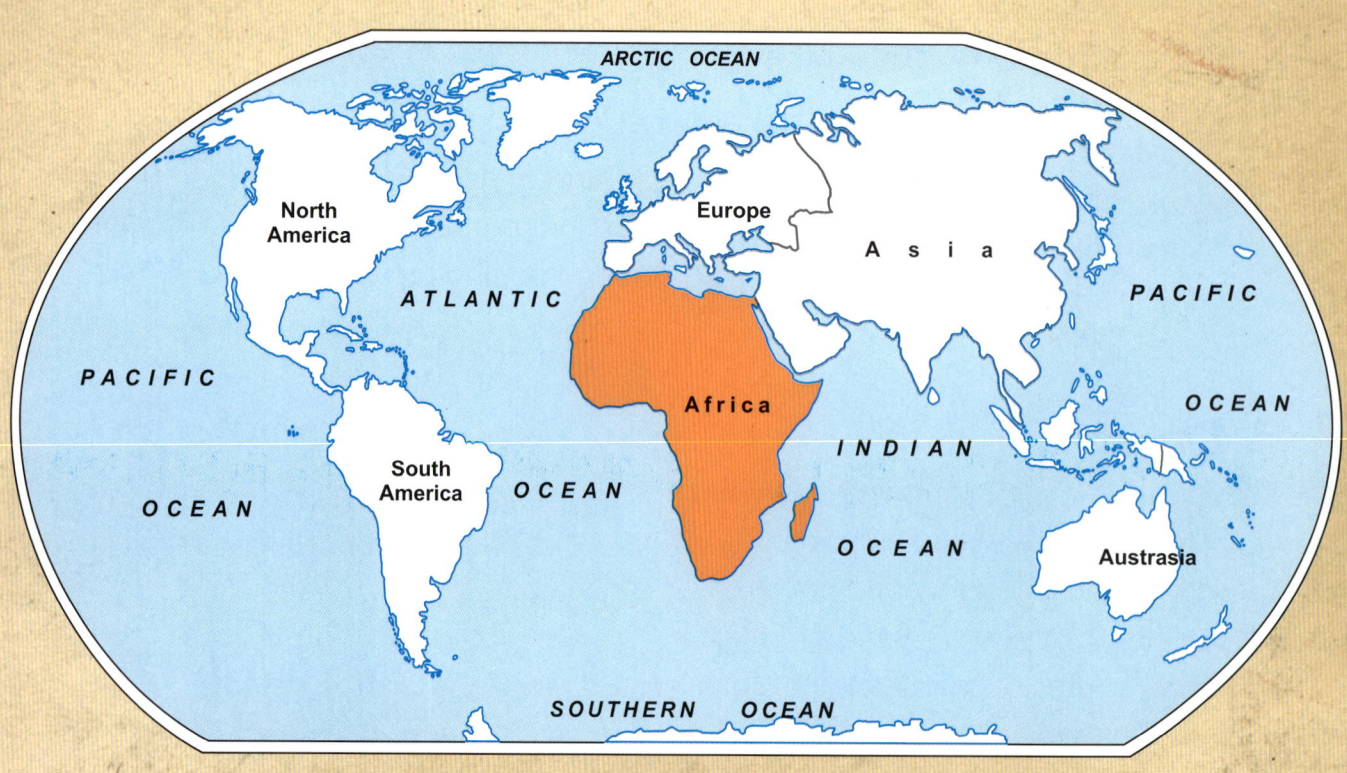

Ancient Africa

Inventions

African people made the earliest and the most important, scientific inventions. The earliest tools, the earliest use of fire and the earliest use of numbers are all from Africa. People in Africa began to make their own stone tools about 1.9 million years ago. Around 60,000 BC, African explorers left Africa and settled in India and Australia, and then West Asia, Europe, and China.

The Africans who stayed behind in Africa began to make fish-hooks, bows and arrows etc. By around 35,000 BC, African people were using tally sticks to keep track of numbers. Women were responsible for the early pottery industry, and also for iron smelting. Both women and men were involved in making African medicine.

Writing

Nobody really knows yet whether the Egyptians invented the art of writing for themselves, or whether they learned it from the Sumerians, who also began writing about the same time, about 3000 BC. The Egyptian form of writing, hieroglyphs, does not look the same or work the same as the Sumerian form of writing, cuneiform. So if they did get the idea from the Sumerians, the Egyptians certainly modified it a lot.

Astonishing fact

The ancient Africans believed in magic amulets. People would visit the village witchdoctor in hopes of finding help for their problems. The witchdoctor may have made them a magic amulet. It is not surprising that the people believed in magic as the amulets often worked!

Ancient African religion

The people in the ancient African villages believed that one god ruled the world, but many gods were in charge of daily life. They believed in two worlds – the world on Earth and the world of the gods. Their religion was designed to bring these two worlds together so that the elders, their religious leaders, could talk to the gods of daily life and receive advice. To encourage these gods to visit them, they danced, sang, rattled noisemakers, made masks and feasted.

ANCIENT HISTORY

Ancestor worship

The ancient Africans also asked their ancestors to talk to the gods on their behalf. They did many things to please their ancestors so that they would make a request on their behalf – things like storytelling and music and song and dance and feasting.

Ancient African Art

The earliest art we know about comes from South Africa, where there are carvings from about 80,000 BC. After that, however, there's a big gap. By about 27,000 BC, people in South Africa, may have been painting pictures of people and animals on rock walls.

African masks

African art

Astonishing fact

The term 'evil eye' is send to have originated in Africa. It is believed to bring harm to the sick and vulnerable.

30

Test Your MEMORY

1. What does the word 'Mesopotamia' mean in Greek?
2. Write a short note on mummification.
3. Who was Tutankhamen? Why is he important in history?
4. What were the Colosseums? For what purpose were they used?
5. Who were the gladiators?
6. When and where was the first Olympic games held?
7. Write a short note on Alexander the Great.
8. Write briefly on any one these ancient stalwarts—Socrates, Aristotle or Plato.
9. Which was the largest and the most powerful state in ancient Greece? Give an account of it briefly.
10. What do you understand by Mesoamerican cultures?
11. Give a brief account of the Chavin culture.
12. Which city is known as the 'lost city' in ancient Arabia?

Index

A
Abu Simbel Temples 13
Akhetaten 14
amulets 29
Assyria 9

B
Babylon 9, 20
black land 10

C
Chavin 23, 24, 31
Colosseum 15, 16
Cuneiform 6

E
Emperor 15, 26

G
Gilgamesh 6
gladiators 17
Great Pyramid 12

H
headdress 12

J
Julius Caesar 16

M
masks 29, 30
Mecca 26
Mesopotamia 4, 5, 8, 25, 31
mosaics 7
mummification 11, 31

N
Nabataeans 25, 26
Nanna 7
Neolithic period 3
Nineveh 9
Nubia 13, 28

O
Olympia 18

P
Pantheon 15
Parthenon 15, 21
Petra 25, 26
Pharaoh Ramesse II 13

R
red land 10

S
Sumer 5, 6, 9

T
The Olmecs 22, 23
The Wooden Horse 19
Tigris 4, 5, 6, 7
Trajan 15, 26
Tutankhamun 14

W
witchdoctor 29

Z
Ziggurat 4, 5